STRIKE UP THE TOEIC® TEST
LISTENING

Yukihiro Tsukada

KINSEIDO

Kinseido Publishing Co., Ltd.
3-21 Kanda Jimbo-cho, Chiyoda-ku,
Tokyo 101-0051, Japan

Copyright © 2015 by Yukihiro Tsukada

All rights reserved. No part of this publication may be reproduced, stored in a retrieval system, or transmitted, in any form or by any means, electronic, mechanical, photocopying, recording or otherwise, without the prior permission of the publisher.

First published 2015 by Kinseido Publishing Co., Ltd.

Cover design　sein
Text design　　guild

この教科書で　DL 00 の表示がある箇所の音声は、上記 URL または QR コードにて無料でダウンロードできます。自習用音声としてご活用ください。

- ▶ PC からのダウンロードをお勧めします。スマートフォンなどでダウンロードされる場合は、ダウンロード前に「解凍アプリ」をインストールしてください。
- ▶ URL は、**検索ボックスではなくアドレスバー (URL 表示覧) に入力**してください。
- ▶ お使いのネットワーク環境によっては、ダウンロードできない場合があります。

CD 00　左記の表示がある箇所の音声は、教室用 CD（Class Audio CD）に収録されています。

はしがき

● TOEIC を学ぶ皆さんへ

TOEIC は、今や大学生や社会人の必須テストです。

日本や韓国を中心に世界 120 カ国で実施され、国内の受験者は年間 200 万人を超えました。

英語コミュニケーション力の認定テストとして、ビジネスの現場や日常生活において、どの程度のコミュニケーション力があるかを測定するのが TOEIC です。最も受験者の多い「公開テスト」と「団体テスト (IP)」では、リスニング (Part 1 〜 4) とリーディング (Part 5 〜 7) が各 100 題 (計 200 題) 出題されます。他に、TOEIC SW テスト (スピーキング／ライティング・テスト) や TOEIC Bridge (初級者向け) があります。

本書は、TOEIC の「リスニング」にターゲットを絞っています。リスニング力を向上させて、ハイスコアを目指しましょう。

●本書の構成

本書は全 24 の UNIT で構成されています。各 UNIT では、TOEIC 頻出のテーマを厳選しました。毎回、Part 1 〜 4 までのリスニングセクションをまるごと学習する構成になっています。

各 Part 学習ステップ

●パターンとテクニックを身につけよう

TOEIC の「リスニング」では、「耳」を鍛えることが大事です。加えて、Part 3 & 4 では、設問と選択肢を読む「リーディング」力も問われます。その能力向上には、テストパターンを把握し、効率良く解答するテクニックが不可欠です。結果、英語力が上がれば言うことなしですね。本書を活用して、TOEIC のスコアアップを目指してください。

塚田幸光

STRIKE UP THE TOEIC® TEST LISTENING　Contents

TOEIC の構成 …… 4
TOEIC パート別攻略ポイント …… 5
切り取り式解答用紙【巻末】

Unit	Title	Page	Part 1	Part 2	Part 3	Part 4
1	Daily Life	14	日常生活	疑問詞	道案内	留守録
2	Restaurant	16	レストラン	ふつうの疑問文	予約の電話	宣伝、広告
3	Party	18	パーティ	疑問詞	オフィスにて	スピーチ
4	Airport	20	空港	提案、勧誘	空港にて	アナウンス
5	Hotel	22	ホテル	選択疑問文	ホテルトラブル	留守録
6	Traffic	24	交通	否定疑問文	交通機関にて	アナウンス
7	Tour & Event	26	イベント	付加疑問文	旅行に関する会話	ニュース
8	Shopping	28	ショッピング	提案、勧誘	店頭にて	宣伝、広告
9	Service	30	サービス	選択疑問文	サービスに関する会話	宣伝、広告
10	Health	32	病院、健康	付加疑問文	予約の電話	留守録
11	Finance & Banking	34	銀行	疑問詞	銀行トラブル	宣伝、広告
12	Housing	36	住宅、不動産	ふつうの疑問文	住まいに関する会話	留守録

Unit	Title	Page	Part 1	Part 2	Part 3	Part 4
13	Media	38	道路状況	平叙文、特殊な文	オフィスにて	ニュース
14	Business	40	ビジネス	特殊な文	オフィスにて	ニュース
15	Reception Desk	42	受付	依頼文	受付にて	自動音声案内
16	Office Work	44	オフィス	依頼文	同僚との会話	スピーチ
17	Employment & Personnel	46	雇用、人事	間接疑問文	人事関連	スピーチ
18	Office Announcement	48	オフィス	平叙文	同僚との会話	アナウンス
19	Office Talk	50	オフィス	平叙文	オフィストラブル	アナウンス
20	New Products	52	新製品	応答が疑問文の場合	新製品に関する会話	宣伝、広告
21	Sales	54	セール	提案、勧誘	店頭にて	宣伝、広告
22	Seminar & Meeting	56	会議	否定疑問文	セミナーに関する会話	スピーチ
23	Logistics	58	運輸	Howを使った文	運輸に関する会話	自動音声案内
24	Construction & Production	60	工事、作業	疑問詞	工事に関する会話	業務連絡

TOEICの構成

リスニングセクション（100問）　解答時間約45分

Part 1 写真描写問題（10問） →詳しい説明や攻略法は6ページ参照	1枚の写真に関する短い4つの英文（選択肢）が放送されます。4つのうち、写真を最も的確に描写しているものを選びます。選択肢は印刷されていません。
Part 2 応答問題（30問） →詳しい説明や攻略法は7ページ参照	1つの問いかけ（質問文）に対し、3つの応答（選択肢）が放送されます。設問に対して最もふさわしい応答を選びます。問いかけも応答も印刷されていません。
Part 3 会話問題（30問） →詳しい説明や攻略法は8ページ参照	2人の人物による会話が放送されます。会話を聞いて問題用紙に印刷された設問と4つの選択肢を読み（設問のみ放送される）、その中から最も適当なものを選びます。各会話には設問が3問ずつあります。会話は印刷されていません。
Part 4 説明文問題（30問） →詳しい説明や攻略法は9ページ参照	アナウンスやナレーションなどの説明文が放送されます。各説明文を聞いて問題用紙に印刷された設問と4つの選択肢を読み（設問のみ放送される）、その中から最も適当なものを選びます。各説明文には設問が3問ずつあります。説明文は印刷されていません。

リーディングセクション（100問）　解答時間約75分

Part 5 短文穴埋め問題（40問） →詳しい説明や攻略法は10ページ参照	不完全な短文の空所を補う語句として、最も適当なものを4つの選択肢の中から選び、文章を完成させます。
Part 6 長文穴埋め問題（12問） →詳しい説明や攻略法は11ページ参照	メールや手紙などの不完全な文章の空所を補う語句として、最も適当なものを4つの選択肢の中から選び、文章を完成させます。
Part 7 読解問題（48問） →詳しい説明や攻略法は12ページ参照	Eメール、社内メモ、広告などの文書とそれに関する設問を読み、4つの選択肢の中から最も適当なものを選びます。全48問中、文書1つを読んで答えるシングル・パッセージ問題が28問、文書2つを読んで答えるダブル・パッセージ問題が20問あります。

TOEIC パート別 攻略ポイント

TOEICでは、限られた時間内で200問という多くの問題を解く必要があります。高いスコアを取るには、ただやみくもに問題を解くのではなく、「戦略」を考えて挑むことが不可欠です。ここでは、パートそれぞれの攻略ポイントを紹介します。試験直前などに、ここをザッと見ておくことをお勧めします。なお、本書では、リスニングセクション（Part 1 〜 Part 4）を扱います。

Part 1 の攻略ポイント

● **形式**

問題数：10問

選択肢数：4つ

所要時間：約5分（問題1問につき約25～30秒）

目標解答時間：1問＝約5秒

注意点：4つの英文（選択肢）は、テスト用紙に印刷されていません

● **攻略ステップ**

ステップ①…写真を見る
Part 1の写真では、「**人物**」と「**風景**」の2パターンが出ます。細かい事柄ではなく、一番「**目立つもの（人）**」をチェックします。

ステップ②…放送を聞く
写真のポイントを把握して、ポイントとなる音を待ち伏せしましょう。チェック・ポイントは以下です。

<人物写真>
1．人数・性別
2．特徴（外見・服装）
3．動作（何をしているか）

<風景写真>
1．場所
2．物（目立つモノ）
3．状態・位置（カタチを見る）

ステップ③…TOEIC的トリックに注意
1．**似ている音**（coffee / copy や car / cart などの似ている音に注意！）
2．**言い換え**（bus でなく vehicle という抽象的な語への言い換えに注意！）
3．**カタチを見抜く**（side by side などの「位置・状態」フレーズが頻出！）

Part 2 の攻略ポイント

● 形式

問題数：30 問
選択肢数：3 つ
所要時間：約 10 分（問題 1 問につき約 20 秒）
目標解答時間：1 問＝約 5 秒
注意点：質問・応答は、テスト用紙に印刷されていません

● 攻略ステップ

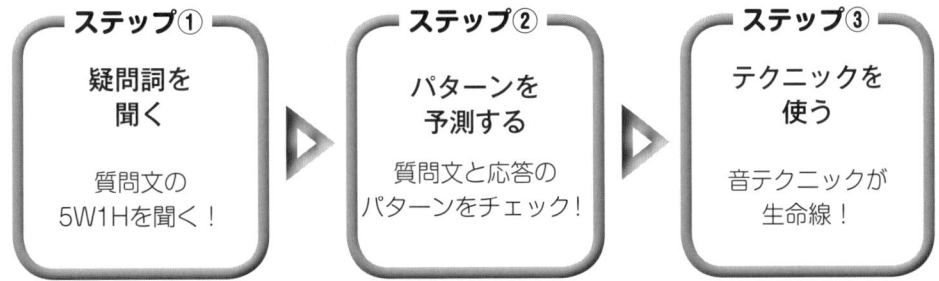

ステップ①…疑問詞を聞く
Part 2 では、**最初の 1 語の聞き取りが最大のポイント**です。**5W1H 疑問詞**（Who, What, When, Where, Why, How）さえわかれば、半分以上が解けます。まずは、「疑問詞」を聞くことから始めましょう。

ステップ②…パターンを予測する
Part 2 は、5W1H 疑問文の他に**7つの質問文パターン**があります。①付加疑問文（..., isn't it?）、②ふつうの疑問文（Do you ...?）、③否定疑問文（Don't you ...?）、④提案・勧誘（Why don't you ...?）、⑤依頼文（Will you ...?）、⑥選択疑問文（A or B?）、⑦平叙文（? マークがないふつうの文）です。それぞれにパターンがあるので、本編で確認しましょう。

ステップ③…テクニックを使う
音のテクニックは、主に 2 つ。Part 2 の定番なのでマスターしましょう。

1. 音の反復は×
   質問文で聞こえた単語が、応答文でも聞こえたら、その選択肢は×。
2. 誤連想も×
   聞こえた音から、関連する単語を（勝手に）連想してはダメ。

Part 3 の攻略ポイント

● 形式

問題数：30問（会話10セット、各会話に設問が3つ）

選択肢数：4つ

所要時間：約14分（「会話＋設問」セット1つが約1分～1分50秒）

目標解答時間：1設問＝約8秒

注意点：設問と選択肢はテスト用紙に印刷されています

● 攻略ステップ

ステップ①…設問を先読みする

設問には2パターンあります。会話文の目的や状況、場所などを問う「主題」に関する設問（＝**「全体」を問う設問**）と、会話文の細部を問う設問（＝**「部分」を問う設問**）です。設問をパッと見て「全体」か「部分」かをチェックします。

ステップ②…設問パターンをチェック！

「全体」を問う設問ならば、**会話の冒頭**を聞けば解答できます。一方、「部分」を問う設問は、チェック・ポイントが2つあります。What will the man do by this afternoon?（男性は今日の午後までに何をしますか）ならば、**設問の「主語」**と**名詞「キーワード」**です。「主語（the man）」は、男女どちらの会話に答えがあるかを示していますし、「キーワード（this afternoon）」はリスニングの聞きどころになります。

ステップ③…ポイントを待ち伏せる

放送を聞く前に、①と②の設問ポイントをチェックします。このチェックがあれば、設問のポイントを待ち伏せた上でのリスニングができるはずです。

Part 4 の攻略ポイント

● **形式**

問題数：30問（説明文10セット、各説明文に設問が3つ）

選択肢数：4つ

所要時間：約16分（「説明文＋設問」セット1つが約1分30秒〜2分）

目標解答時間：1設問＝約8秒

注意点：設問と選択肢はテスト用紙に印刷されています

● **攻略ステップ**

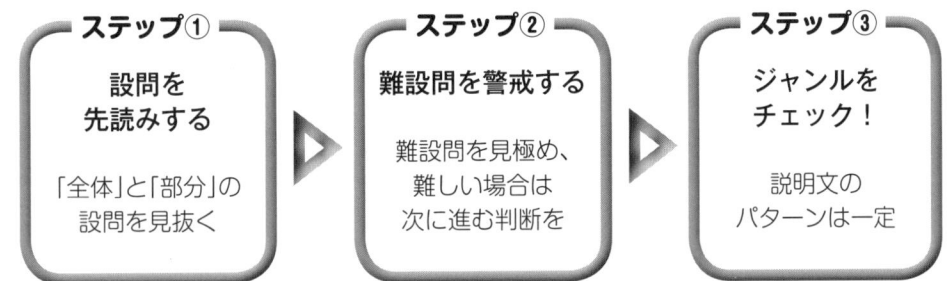

ステップ①…設問を先読みする

Part 3と同じく、まず「全体」と「部分」の設問をチェックします。「全体」ならば、冒頭に集中して、主題をつかめばOK。「部分」はキーワードをチェックして、ポイントを待ち伏せします。

ステップ②…難設問を警戒する

Part 4の説明文は、かなり長いので、リスニングの持久力が試されます。当然、全部を把握するのは大変なことです。そして難設問を避けるのも戦略です。これに時間をかけると、解けるものを逃すことにもなりかねません。難設問のポイントは3つ。① probably や likely を含む設問、② Why の設問の他に、③ 3つの「i」を含む設問（imply, indicate, infer）があります。

ステップ③…ジャンルをチェック！

Part 4では、説明文のジャンルが決まっています。①**スピーチ**（受賞・紹介スピーチ）、②**アナウンス**（社内・公共アナウンス）、③**ニュース**（交通・ビジネスニュース）、④**広告**（セール案内、ラジオCM）、⑤**ツアーガイド**、⑥**電話**（留守録、自動音声ガイド）。これらの説明文には、パターンがある点も重要です。

Part 5 の攻略ポイント

● 形式

問題数：40問

選択肢数：4つ

目標解答時間：1問＝約30秒（全体で20分以内）

● 攻略ステップ

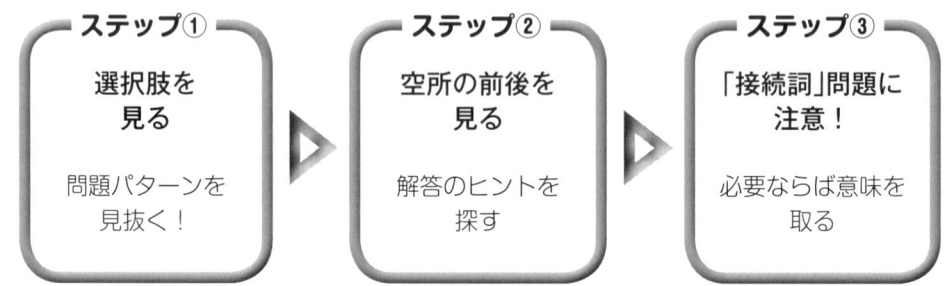

ステップ①…選択肢を見る
Part 5では、まず選択肢を見ます。以下のパターンから問題を把握します。
1．選択肢の品詞がバラバラな場合→「品詞問題」
2．選択肢の品詞に共通点がある場合→「文法問題」もしくは「語彙問題」

ステップ②…空所の前後を見る
空所の前後を見て、解答のヒントを探します。意味を取るのではなく、カタチを見ることが大事！
1．「品詞問題」→空所の品詞を見抜けばOK
2．「文法問題」→空所の前後に「文法ヒント」を探す
　　例えば、recently があるときは、空所は過去形か現在完了形。
3．「語彙問題」→空所の前後に「フレーズのカップリング」を探す
　　例えば、office (supplies) や (issue) a warning といった組み合わせ。

ステップ③…「接続詞」問題に注意！
Part 5では、①②のポイントで「意味ではなくカタチから解く」のが大事です。ただし例外はいくつかあります。その代表格が「接続詞」問題。文構造と意味の両方から解く必要があります。

Part 6 の攻略ポイント

● 形式

問題数：12問（長文4セット）
選択肢数：4つ
目標解答時間：1長文（3問）＝2分以内（全体で8分以内）

● 攻略ステップ

ステップ①…ジャンルをチェック！
Part 6 では、メール、記事、広告などの文書が出題されます。内容はセミナーの招待文や支払いの通知などのビジネス文書です。ジャンルをチェックしておけば、ステップ③の文脈問題で有利になり、ジャンル特有の定型文にも対応できます。例えば、Please (accept) our apologies for making the mistake.（不手際をおわびいたします）。空所の accept は、定型文を知っていれば簡単ですね。

ステップ②…選択肢と空所を見る
Part 6 の大半の問題は、Part 5 と同じです。選択肢を見て、「品詞」「文法」「語彙」問題を見極め、空所の前後を見て、即答しましょう。

ステップ③…「文脈」問題に注意！
Part 6 の難所は、「文脈」問題です。パターンは4つ。「時制」、「接続副詞」(However など）、「代名詞」、「語彙」です。空所の前後だけでは解けず、広い範囲を読まねばなりません。この**文脈4パターン**を見たら、警戒する必要があるでしょう。

Part 7 の攻略ポイント

● 形式

問題数：48 問
　シングル・パッセージ：文書 9、設問数 28 問
　ダブル・パッセージ：文書 4 セット（文書計 8）、設問数 20 問
目標解答時間：1 問 1 分（全体で 48 分以内）

● 攻略ステップ

ステップ①…ジャンルをチェック！
Part 7 では、特定のジャンルの文書が出題されます。その内容も一定なので、パターンを把握しておくと有利です。ジャンルには「**メール**」、「**手紙**」、「**広告**」、「**通知**」、「**記事**」、「**プレスリリース**」、「**フォーム**」、「**説明書**」などがあります。

ステップ②…設問をチェック！
Part 3 & 4 と同じく、設問にはパターンがあります。「全体」を問う設問、「部分」を問う設問、「難」設問をチェックしましょう。特に「難」設問は、3 つの「i」を含む設問（indicate, imply, infer）に加え、本文と選択肢の比較検討が必要な「NOT を含む設問」（NOT 問題）が要注意です。また、ダブル・パッセージ問題では、2 つの文書両方からヒントを拾う「クロス・リファレンス」問題も出題されます。

ステップ③…サーチ&ファインド！
Part 7 の標準解答時間は、1 問 1 分です。文章をゆっくり読んでいる時間はありません。設問の該当箇所をサーチ&ファインドして、即答しましょう。

Unit 1
Daily Life

TOEICではビジネスだけでなく、日常生活に関するトピックも多く出題されます。電話表現や道案内のやりとりを中心に基本事項をチェックしましょう。

Part 1 Photographs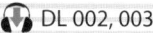

Look at the picture and choose the statement that best describes what you see.

1. (A) (B) (C) (D)　　　　　　　　　**2.** (A) (B) (C) (D)

「動作」を聞こう！
まずは、動詞に
耳を澄まして！

人物が
何をしているかを
チェック！

Part 2 Question-Response

Choose the best response to each question or statement.

3. (A)　(B)　(C)
4. (A)　(B)　(C)
5. (A)　(B)　(C)
6. (A)　(B)　(C)

まず、「疑問詞」を聞こう！
最初の1語に集中！

Part 3　Short Conversations

Listen to a short conversation, and choose the best answer to each question.

7. Why does the man not know the way to the station?
   (A) He forgot his map of the train system.
   (B) He is too tired to look around.
   (C) He is unfamiliar with the city.
   (D) He does not know the name.

   設問の「主語」を
   チェックしよう！
   男女のセリフのどちらに
   答えがあるかわかる！

8. What is in front of the station?
   (A) A police station　(C) A big sign
   (B) A flower shop　(D) A taxi stand

   「位置」関係を把握しよう！

9. What does the woman say city residents enjoy doing?
   (A) Operating their own businesses
   (B) Assisting people whenever they can
   (C) Traveling to faraway destinations
   (D) Searching for a large sign

   選択肢の「タテ読み」！
   意味をさっとチェック！

Part 4　Short Talks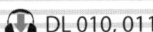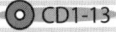

Listen to a short talk, and choose the best answer to each question.

10. What kind of company is GP Union Electric?
    (A) Social services
    (B) A labor union
    (C) A repair company
    (D) An appliance store

    「どんな会社」→ 選択肢４つを「タテ読み」！

11. Why is Travis Samuel calling?
    (A) To ask for a monetary donation
    (B) To verify customer satisfaction
    (C) To publicize a new company service
    (D) To offer a free upgrade coupon

    「タテ読み」を有効に使おう！
    ここでは電話した理由が
    問われている

12. According to the speaker, how can the listener report problems?
    (A) By writing a letter
    (B) By visiting the company
    (C) By sending back the questionnaire
    (D) By participating in a survey

    〈How→By〉のパターンは定番！
    説明文の後半にヒント！

Unit **1** Daily Life　15

Unit 2

Restaurant

レストランでは、テーブルの予約、キャンセル、注文のやりとりが定番です。
シチュエーションをイメージして、関連表現を覚えましょう。

Part 1 Photographs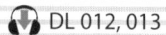

Look at the picture and choose the statement that best describes what you see.

1. (A) (B) (C) (D)   2. (A) (B) (C) (D)

人物の「共通点」を
チェック！
2人はどうしてる？

「空席」は
何て言う？
「状態」を見よう！

Part 2 Question-Response

Choose the best response to each question or statement.

3. (A) (B) (C)
4. (A) (B) (C)   トリッキーな応答に
5. (A) (B) (C)   注意しよう
6. (A) (B) (C)

Part 3 Short Conversations 🎧 DL 018, 019  ~

Listen to a short conversation, and choose the best answer to each question.

7. Why is the woman calling?
   (A) To order a set menu
   (B) To cancel an event
   (C) To book a flight
   (D) To find a place for a party

   > 電話の「理由」は、I'm calling が「耳印」!

8. What does the man say about dates?
   (A) None are available.
   (B) There are two days to choose from.
   (C) The 15th is reserved.
   (D) Dates are all set.

   > 「日付」はくせ者！ダミー日付に惑わされるな！

9. What does the woman decide to do?
   (A) Call again in December
   (B) Have a 4-hour party
   (C) Make a tentative reservation
   (D) Pay a cancellation charge

   > セオリー通り「主語」をチェック！

Part 4 Short Talks 🎧 DL 020, 021  ~

Listen to a short talk, and choose the best answer to each question.

10. What type of business is being advertised?
    (A) A bank   (C) A travel agency
    (B) A law office   (D) A restaurant

    > 「広告」のジャンルを見抜け！

11. What are the opening times?
    (A) Morning to late at night   (C) Just lunchtimes
    (B) Afternoon to night   (D) Evenings only

    > 店舗の「開店時間」は open が「耳印」

12. How can listeners reserve a space?
    (A) By talking to the client
    (B) By making an online reservation
    (C) By telephoning the establishment
    (D) By turning up at 9 a.m.

    > 〈How→By〉パターン！説明文の後半に集中！

Unit **2** Restaurant   17

Unit 3

Party

TOEICは大のパーティ好き。会社主催のオフィスパーティに加え、歓迎会や送別会もよく出ます。パーティに関するやりとりに慣れましょう。

Part 1　Photographs　　DL 022, 023　　CD1-32　　CD1-33

Look at the picture and choose the statement that best describes what you see.

1. (A) (B) (C) (D)　　　　2. (A) (B) (C) (D)

人物の「特徴」を
チェック！
外見・服装は？

風景写真では
「目立つもの」を
見よう！

Part 2　Question-Response　　DL 024～027　　CD1-34 ～　CD1-37

Choose the best response to each question or statement.

3. (A)　(B)　(C)
4. (A)　(B)　(C)　　「音の反復」は不正解！
5. (A)　(B)　(C)　　音テクをマスターして！
6. (A)　(B)　(C)

Part 3 Short Conversations 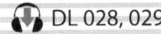  ~

Listen to a short conversation, and choose the best answer to each question.

7. Where most likely are the speakers?
   (A) On a golf course
   (B) At a company
   (C) On a mountain
   (D) At a party

   > 話し手の「場所」を問う定番！
   > 冒頭の数秒にヒント！

8. Who is Gordon?
   (A) A school friend
   (B) An old client
   (C) An office superior
   (D) A new worker

   > Who 設問では、
   > 「職業」「職種」が問われる！

9. What is being planned?
   (A) A golf trip
   (B) An overseas visit
   (C) A farewell party
   (D) A mountain trek

   > TOEIC は
   > イベント好き！

Part 4 Short Talks 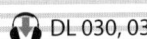  ~

Listen to a short talk, and choose the best answer to each question.

10. How long has Jennifer Howell been working for Central Electric?
    (A) For two years
    (B) For three years
    (C) For five years
    (D) For fifteen years

    > 「勤務年数」はよく出る！
    > 冒頭の数字をキャッチせよ！

11. What does Jennifer Howell do now?
    (A) She has retired from Central Electric.
    (B) She is the General Manager at the Windsor branch.
    (C) She works in the customer service department.
    (D) She is the head of all the business in part of the country.

    > now がポイント！
    > 彼女の今の役職は？

12. What will the speaker most likely do next?
    (A) Ask Jennifer Howell to make a speech
    (B) Make a phone call to General Manager
    (C) Work to restore power to all customers
    (D) Enjoy some food and beverages

    > do next を見たら、
    > 本文の一番最後にヒント！

Unit 3 Party   19

Unit 4

Airport

空港は頻出シチュエーション。送迎トピックに加え、様々なトラブル・トピックに注意しましょう。なかでも、飛行機の「遅延」は毎回出ます。

Part 1　Photographs　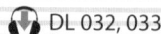

Look at the picture and choose the statement that best describes what you see.

1. (A) (B) (C) (D)　　　　　　　　2. (A) (B) (C) (D)

Part 2　Question-Response　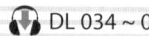

Choose the best response to each question or statement.

3. (A)　(B)　(C)
4. (A)　(B)　(C)
5. (A)　(B)　(C)
6. (A)　(B)　(C)

Part 3 Short Conversations   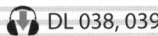  ~

Listen to a short conversation, and choose the best answer to each question.

7. Who most likely is the woman?
   - (A) A flight attendant
   - (B) An airline staff
   - (C) A travel agent
   - (D) A secretary

   定番の Who 設問！
   冒頭からシチュエーションを把握すれば簡単！

8. When will the man arrive?
   - (A) At 2:00 p.m.
   - (B) At 4:00 p.m.
   - (C) At 6:00 p.m.
   - (D) At 7:00 p.m.

   When 設問は、意外と「難」！
   ダミー時間に注意して！

9. Why does the man prefer the flight with the layover?
   - (A) He will arrive earlier.
   - (B) He hates bad weather.
   - (C) He wants to visit Chicago.
   - (D) He has to attend the meeting.

   選択肢の「名詞キーワード」をチェック！
   これを耳印にして、本文を聞こう！

Part 4 Short Talks   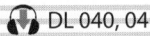  ~

Listen to a short talk, and choose the best answer to each question.

10. Where is this announcement being made?
    - (A) At a hotel
    - (B) At an airport
    - (C) At a station
    - (D) At a theater

    アナウンスの「場所」もよく出る！
    冒頭の数秒で勝負が決まるぞ！

11. Why is the flight canceled?
    - (A) Some passengers have to stay at hotels.
    - (B) Some coupons have been lost.
    - (C) An airplane needs to be fixed.
    - (D) There are too many customers.

    フライトキャンセルの理由は定番！

12. What are listeners asked to do?
    - (A) Remain where they are
    - (B) Get additional information from staff
    - (C) Give out free vouchers
    - (D) Find hotels by themselves

    アナウンスの「お願い文」にヒント！

Unit 4 Airport

Unit 5
Hotel

ホテルも頻出のシチュエーションです。フロントでの予約、キャンセル、支払いに加え、クリーニングなどのルームサービスやトラブルもよく出ます。

Part 1　Photographs

Look at the picture and choose the statement that best describes what you see.

1. (A) (B) (C) (D)　　　2. (A) (B) (C) (D)

Part 2　Question-Response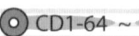

Choose the best response to each question or statement.

3. (A)　(B)　(C)
4. (A)　(B)　(C)
5. (A)　(B)　(C)
6. (A)　(B)　(C)

Part 3　Short Conversations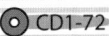

Listen to a short conversation, and choose the best answer to each question.

7. Where is the conversation taking place?
   (A) At a travel agency
   (B) At an international airport
   (C) At a shopping center
   (D) At a resort hotel

   会話の「場所」を問う定番！
   冒頭を聞けばＯＫ！

8. What is wrong with Room 502?
   (A) It doesn't have a beach view.
   (B) There is no parking space.
   (C) The balcony is too big.
   (D) It's too far to the beach.

   ホテルトラブルは必ず出る！
   トラブルに注意！

9. What does the woman offer to do?
   (A) Arrange a new table　　(C) Give a refund
   (B) Provide another room　(D) Check the website

   女性の「申し出」を聞こう

Part 4　Short Talks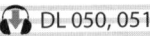

Listen to a short talk, and choose the best answer to each question.

10. Who most likely is the listener of this message?
   (A) A current guest　　(C) A secretary
   (B) A cleaning person　(D) A board director

   電話メッセージの
   「聞き手」は誰？
   こちらも冒頭にヒント！

11. What type of room does Mr. Collins usually have?
   (A) One with a view of the pool
   (B) One on the 8th floor
   (C) One close to the lobby
   (D) One with easy access to the rooftop pool

   いつも泊まっている部屋は？
   usuallyに注目しよう

12. What does the speaker want the listener to do?
   (A) Cancel the visit
   (B) Telephone back soon
   (C) Book the room earlier
   (D) Change the direction

   wantの設問は、Please / Would you～？にヒント！

Unit **5** Hotel　23

Unit 6
Traffic

交通トピックは、道路の状況把握がカギとなります。駐車、渋滞、工事など、様々なケースに対応しなければなりません。関連表現をしっかり覚えましょう。

Part 1　Photographs　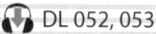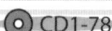

Look at the picture and choose the statement that best describes what you see.

1. (A) (B) (C) (D)　　　　　　　　2. (A) (B) (C) (D)

「一列に駐車」は何て言う？

「同じ方向」もよく出るぞ！

Part 2　Question-Response　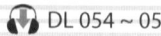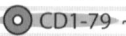

Choose the best response to each question or statement.

3. (A) (B) (C)
4. (A) (B) (C)
5. (A) (B) (C)
6. (A) (B) (C)

「否定疑問文」では、Didn't you = Did you のように考えよう

Part 3 Short Conversations

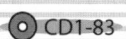

Listen to a short conversation, and choose the best answer to each question.

7. What is the woman's problem?
(A) There are no tickets left.
(B) The train has departed.
(C) She bought the wrong ticket.
(D) The machine is out of order.

「トラブル」を
キャッチしよう！

8. When will the woman probably be returning?
(A) On the same day
(B) The day after tomorrow
(C) In less than a week
(D) After several weeks

選択肢の
「言い換え」に注意！

9. What does the man say he will do?
(A) Give her a one-way ticket
(B) Charge more money
(C) Offer an open ticket
(D) Fix the machine

will do＝will do next
会話の最後にヒント！

Part 4 Short Talks

Listen to a short talk, and choose the best answer to each question.

10. Where does this announcement most likely take place?
(A) In an airport   (C) In a subway car
(B) In a bus station   (D) In a traffic report

アナウンスの「場所」
→冒頭に集中！

11. What does the speaker suggest people going to City Central do to avoid delays?
(A) Wait until they stop
(B) Get off and walk
(C) Use the Blue Line
(D) Avoid the Yellow Line

具体的な箇所をチェック！
これが耳印になる！

12. Why is the public transportation clean in Laurelton?
(A) Eating and drinking is not allowed.
(B) Users throw away refuse properly.
(C) Sanitation workers have been recently hired.
(D) The station staff collects rubbish.

地名＝名詞キーワード！
キーワードを待ち伏せよう

Unit **6** Traffic   25

Unit 7

Tour & Event

旅行やイベント関連のトピックはおなじみですね。チケットの予約・キャンセル、ツアーガイドによる案内、ホテルを会場とするイベントなどが頻出です。

Part 1　Photographs　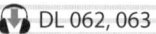

Look at the picture and choose the statement that best describes what you see.

1. (A) (B) (C) (D)　　　　2. (A) (B) (C) (D)

「音楽を演奏する」は何て言う？

人物の「状態」も出る！

Part 2　Question-Response　

Choose the best response to each question or statement.

3. (A)　(B)　(C)
4. (A)　(B)　(C)
5. (A)　(B)　(C)
6. (A)　(B)　(C)

「付加疑問文」の文尾 (aren't you?など) は無視しよう

Part 3 Short Conversations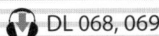

Listen to a short conversation, and choose the best answer to each question.

7. Why is the woman calling?
   (A) To sell an optional tour
   (B) To request some information
   (C) To confirm a schedule
   (D) To renew a travel document

   > 電話の「要件」！
   > 冒頭の数秒を聞こう！

8. What does the man want to do?
   (A) Take part in an extra activity
   (B) Receive some more pamphlets
   (C) Change the date of a visit
   (D) Invite more friends

   > 男性の「要望」は何？
   > would like toの箇所がヒント！

9. When will the cruise most likely be reserved?
   (A) Within a month
   (B) On a rainy day
   (C) The end of next year
   (D) After getting to the location

   > reserve＝bookの
   > 言い換えは定番！

Part 4 Short Talks

Listen to a short talk, and choose the best answer to each question.

10. What is the purpose of the radio announcement?
    (A) To give a weather forecast
    (B) To announce changes in the park schedule
    (C) To talk about the most popular event in the city
    (D) To ask for volunteers to set up booths and stalls

    > アナウンスの「目的」は
    > 冒頭に集中！

11. Where is the Pumpkin Parade held every year?
    (A) In Pumpkin Park   (C) In Jefferson Park
    (B) In City Park   (D) In Middleton Park

    > パレードの「場所」は、
    > heldのあとを聞こう！

12. According to the speaker, what will happen this month?
    (A) A performance will take place.
    (B) The park will be decorated.
    (C) Booths and stalls will be removed.
    (D) Volunteers will clean the event site.

Unit 7 Tour & Event

Unit 8

Shopping

日常生活のなかでもショッピングは定番トピックです。ショッピングのお誘いや商品をめぐるやりとりなど、出題ポイントは決まっています。

Part 1　Photographs

Look at the picture and choose the statement that best describes what you see.

1. (A) (B) (C) (D)　　　　　　　　**2.** (A) (B) (C) (D)

「一列に陳列」は何て言う？

商品の「展示」は必ず出る！

Part 2　Question-Response

Choose the best response to each question or statement.

3. (A)　(B)　(C)
4. (A)　(B)　(C)
5. (A)　(B)　(C)
6. (A)　(B)　(C)

「提案・勧誘」の応答はくせ者が多い！

Part 3 Short Conversations

Listen to a short conversation, and choose the best answer to each question.

7. Where are the two speakers?
   (A) At a design office
   (B) At an accessory boutique
   (C) At a grocery store
   (D) At a supply warehouse

   会話の「場所」！
   セオリー通り、冒頭を聞こう！

8. What does the woman say about her mother?
   (A) Her favorite color is beige.
   (B) Her birthday was last week.
   (C) She loves a certain designer.
   (D) She knows the artist personally.

   motherをキーワードとして、
   その周辺をチェック！

9. What will the man probably do next?
   (A) Telephone to check the stock
   (B) Talk to the woman's mother
   (C) Order a beige product
   (D) Contact the designer directly

   do nextを見たら、
   I'll ~のあとにヒント！

Part 4 Short Talks

Listen to a short talk, and choose the best answer to each question.

10. What will happen on Saturday this week?
    (A) An eating establishment will close.
    (B) There'll be a huge sale.
    (C) A new commercial facility will open.
    (D) A band will split up.

    冒頭から、何が起こるかを
    キャッチしよう

11. Who is Riley Desiree?
    (A) A manager   (C) A councilor
    (B) An actress   (D) A musician

    Who設問＝「職業」！

12. Where will the music entertainment take place?
    (A) On the website
    (B) At the theater complex
    (C) In the restaurant zone
    (D) In the main plaza

    音楽祭の「場所」はどこ？

Unit 8 Shopping   29

Unit 9
Service

TOEICではサービス業務が頻出です。店頭の会話、セール案内、ラジオ広告等々。クレームのトピックが多いのも特徴です。

Part 1　Photographs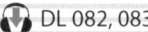

Look at the picture and choose the statement that best describes what you see.

1. (A) (B) (C) (D)　　　　　　　　**2.** (A) (B) (C) (D)

共通点がない場合は、「動作」に集中！

「手を伸ばす」は頻出！

Part 2　Question-Response

Choose the best response to each question or statement.

3. (A)　(B)　(C)
4. (A)　(B)　(C)
5. (A)　(B)　(C)
6. (A)　(B)　(C)

選択疑問文の応答は、イレギュラーが多いぞ！

Part 3 Short Conversations   ~

Listen to a short conversation, and choose the best answer to each question.

7. What is the purpose of the call?
- (A) To check some local news
- (B) To arrange a safety check
- (C) To book a job interview
- (D) To rent a room

> 電話の「目的」！
> セオリー通り、冒頭を聞こう！

8. When is the woman available?
- (A) Monday to Friday
- (B) Sunday afternoon
- (C) Saturday morning
- (D) Weekdays only

> availableの
> ニュアンスを知ろう！

9. How long will the visit take?
- (A) A few minutes
- (B) Ten minutes
- (C) Thirty minutes
- (D) About an hour

> 「期間」→ 選択肢の
> 言い換えに注意！

Part 4 Short Talks    ~

Listen to a short talk, and choose the best answer to each question.

10. What is the purpose of the advertisement?
- (A) To publicize new luxury seats
- (B) To list holiday closing times
- (C) To announce the winner of a contest
- (D) To talk about a new bus route campaign

> 広告の「目的」！
> 冒頭にヒント！

11. What kind of services are available on Apple Bus?
- (A) TV
- (B) Full reclining seats
- (C) Free drink bar
- (D) Internet access

> サービスの
> 種類は何だろう？

12. When does the discount offer end?
- (A) In fifty days
- (B) In half an hour
- (C) In four weeks
- (D) In ten days

> 「割引期間」はよく出る！

Unit **9** Service

Unit 10
Health

健康関連のトピックは、意外な盲点かもしれません。病院の予約・キャンセルに加え、オフィスでは健康診断の案内、スポーツクラブへの参加などが定番です。

Part 1 Photographs

Look at the picture and choose the statement that best describes what you see.

1. (A) (B) (C) (D)   2. (A) (B) (C) (D)

医者が患者を「診る」は何て言う？

女性の指先に注目！

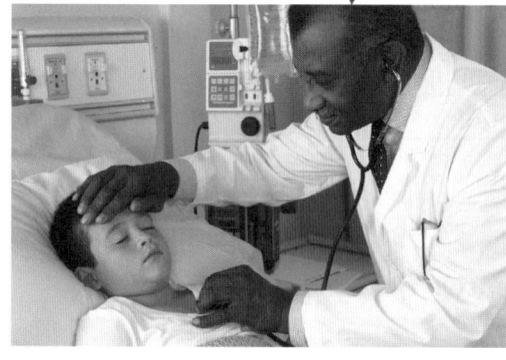
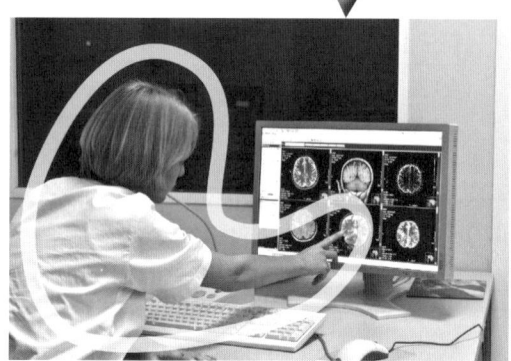

Part 2 Question-Response

Choose the best response to each question or statement.

3. (A)　(B)　(C)
4. (A)　(B)　(C)
5. (A)　(B)　(C)
6. (A)　(B)　(C)

付加疑問文の文末は無視！

Part 3 Short Conversations   DL 098, 099   CD2-53 ~ CD2-57

Listen to a short conversation, and choose the best answer to each question.

7. What is the purpose of the telephone call?
- (A) To confirm a trip
- (B) To make an appointment
- (C) To join a course
- (D) To open an account

> 電話の「目的」！
> セオリー通り、最初に注意！

8. What does the woman request additionally?
- (A) A free drink
- (B) To go alone
- (C) An extra test
- (D) A monthly report

> 女性の
> 「追加」リクエストとは？

9. When will the woman most likely visit the clinic?
- (A) Tomorrow afternoon
- (B) This week
- (C) Next Tuesday
- (D) Wednesday morning

> When 設問はくせ者が多い！
> ひっかけに注意しよう

Part 4 Short Talks   DL 100, 101   CD2-58 ~ CD2-61

Listen to a short talk, and choose the best answer to each question.

10. Where does the speaker probably work?
- (A) In a dental clinic
- (B) In a drug store
- (C) In a medical laboratory
- (D) At a cleaning service

> シチュエーションを推測しよう！

11. What happened this morning?
- (A) A tooth was extracted.
- (B) The office opened late.
- (C) A patient didn't show up for a check-up.
- (D) Someone visited a hospital.

> 「出来事」＝
> 「トラブル」が多いぞ！

12. What is the earliest that the listener can come again?
- (A) This evening after 7 p.m.
- (B) Sometime this week
- (C) After the weekend
- (D) After next week

> 一番早く来れる日は？
> 「予約日」に
> 耳をすませよう

Unit **10** Health

Unit 11
Finance & Banking

銀行はマイナー・トピック。通常のサービス表現がわかれば対応できます。
財務関係は、リーディングは難所ですが、リスニングはそれほど難しくありません。

Part 1　Photographs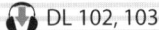

Look at the picture and choose the statement that best describes what you see.

1. (A) (B) (C) (D)　　　　2. (A) (B) (C) (D)

Part 2　Question-Response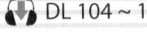

Choose the best response to each question or statement.

3. (A)　(B)　(C)
4. (A)　(B)　(C)
5. (A)　(B)　(C)
6. (A)　(B)　(C)

34

Part 3 Short Conversations   DL 108, 109   CD2-68 ~ CD2-72

Listen to a short conversation, and choose the best answer to each question.

7. Where is the conversation taking place? 〔会話の「場所」→ 冒頭！〕
   (A) In an IT department
   (B) In a hotel lobby
   (C) In a financial institute
   (D) In an insurance firm

8. What is the man's problem? 〔「トラブル」をキャッチしよう！〕
   (A) He can't get money.
   (B) The worker hasn't been paid.
   (C) The ATM isn't open.
   (D) His card was stolen.

〔go next → 会話の最後に集中！〕

9. Where will the man most likely go next?
   (A) The department store   (C) The teller counter
   (B) The cash dispenser   (D) The vending machine

Part 4 Short Talks   DL 110, 111   CD2-73 ~ CD2-76

Listen to a short talk, and choose the best answer to each question.

10. Who is this advertisement aimed at? 〔広告のターゲットは誰？冒頭から推測しよう！〕
   (A) First-time customers   (C) Bank employees
   (B) Users for over 5 years   (D) Overseas travelers

11. What service is being offered? 〔どんな「サービス」？ offer のあとにヒント！〕
   (A) Competitive exchange rates
   (B) Free financial advice
   (C) High interest time deposit
   (D) Special spending discounts

12. How should listeners apply for the offer? 〔〈How→By〉のパターン！ウェブでの申込が正解になりやすい〕
   (A) By checking the newspaper for details
   (B) By going online to register
   (C) By sending an application form
   (D) By waiting at least one year

Unit **11** Finance & Banking   35

Unit 12

Housing

住まい関連のトピックは意外とよく出ます。不動産屋とのやりとりでは、空き部屋情報や家賃、新築物件の見学案内など、大人な会話も頻出です。

Part 1 Photographs   DL 112, 113   CD2-77   CD2-78

Look at the picture and choose the statement that best describes what you see.

1. (A) (B) (C) (D)   2. (A) (B) (C) (D)

「位置・状態」を把握しよう！

「見下ろす」はよく出る！

Part 2 Question-Response   DL 114～117   CD2-79 ～ CD2-82

Choose the best response to each question or statement.

3. (A) (B) (C)
4. (A) (B) (C)
5. (A) (B) (C)
6. (A) (B) (C)

応答の「省略」に慣れよう！

Part 3 Short Conversations   DL 118, 119   CD2-83 ~ CD2-87

Listen to a short conversation, and choose the best answer to each question.

7. Who most likely is the woman?
   (A) A hotel receptionist
   (B) A construction builder
   (C) A real estate agent
   (D) A housekeeper

   > 女性の「職業」を冒頭から推測！

8. What does the man ask for?
   (A) A room with a great view
   (B) 3 separate bedrooms
   (C) A location closer to the workplace
   (D) A spacious room

   > 男性の「要望」を聞こう！

9. What will probably happen after this?
   (A) The apartment will be renovated.
   (B) The man will visit the property.
   (C) The room will be shared.
   (D) The price will be reduced.

   > after this はこのあとの展開！
   > → 最後を聞けば OK

Part 4 Short Talks   DL 120, 121   CD2-88 ~ CD2-91

Listen to a short talk, and choose the best answer to each question.

10. Who most likely is the listener?
    (A) A real-estate agent
    (B) An office worker
    (C) A parking attendant
    (D) A security guard

    > メッセージの「聞き手」を推測しよう！

11. According to the speaker, what has the listener requested?
    (A) A convenient residence
    (B) A private terraced house
    (C) A self-catering hotel room
    (D) A country bungalow

    > 聞き手の「要望」は？
    > 部屋のタイプを聞き逃すな！

12. When will the listener be in the area next?
    (A) The listener is already there
    (B) When the branch opens
    (C) Sometime next week
    (D) In about 5 minutes

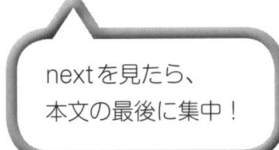

    > next を見たら、本文の最後に集中！

Unit **12** Housing   37

Unit 13
Media

ニュース関連は、交通情報を筆頭に、ビジネスニュースや新製品の紹介などが出題されます。ニュースは語彙が難しいので、リスニング最大の難所です。

Part 1　Photographs　　DL 122, 123　CD3-02　CD3-03

Look at the picture and choose the statement that best describes what you see.

1. (A) (B) (C) (D)　　　　2. (A) (B) (C) (D)

交通の定型表現が出る！

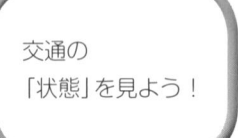

交通の「状態」を見よう！

Part 2　Question-Response　　DL 124 ~ 127　CD3-04 ~ CD3-07

Choose the best response to each question or statement.

3. (A) (B) (C)
4. (A) (B) (C)
5. (A) (B) (C)
6. (A) (B) (C)

質問文が「平叙文（ふつうの文）」のときは難問が多い！

Part 3 Short Conversations   DL 128, 129   CD3-08 ~ CD3-12

Listen to a short conversation, and choose the best answer to each question.

7. What is the news saying about next week?
   (A) A new budget will be made.
   (B) The exchange rate will go down.
   (C) The Euro will be stronger.
   (D) The number of employees will increase.

   > ニュースの主題を聞き取ろう！
   > 当然、冒頭に集中！

8. What problem does the woman mention?
   (A) The office is going to move.
   (B) Import costs will rise.
   (C) Some machine parts are left.
   (D) An overseas visitor is coming.

   > トラブル／問題
   > →「マイナス」要素をキャッチ！

9. What will the woman suggest the company do?
   (A) Buy Euros this week
   (B) Temporarily stop ordering the parts
   (C) Cut down the budget
   (D) Import products next month

   > 女性の「提案」を聞こう！
   > suggestは「難」設問のサイン！

Part 4 Short Talks   DL 130, 131   CD3-13 ~ CD3-16

Listen to a short talk, and choose the best answer to each question.

10. What is the main topic of the news report?
    (A) The result of the campaign
    (B) The birth of a new cub
    (C) The renaming of the zoo
    (D) The dates of the event

    > ニュースの「主題」は何？
    > 名詞キーワード＝耳印！

11. According to the report, what happened eight years ago?
    (A) The zoo was founded.
    (B) The panda got older.
    (C) A panda cub was born.
    (D) Zoo officials named the cub.

12. Why should visitors to the zoo come early?
    (A) The weather is inclement.
    (B) Many guests are expected.
    (C) The number of tickets is limited.
    (D) The zoo closes early.

    > Why設問に注意！
    > 「理由」のキャッチは予想外に難しい

Unit 14
Business

ビジネスは TOEIC の代名詞。会議トークやスピーチ、合併協議や商品発注など話題は多岐に及びます。仕事のシチュエーション把握がスコアアップの近道です。

Part 1　Photographs　 DL 132, 133　CD3-17　CD3-18

Look at the picture and choose the statement that best describes what you see.

1. (A) (B) (C) (D)　　　　　　　　2. (A) (B) (C) (D)

「物が積まれている」は何て言う？

人物の「動作」をチェック！

Part 2　Question-Response　 DL 134～137　CD3-19 ～ CD3-22

Choose the best response to each question or statement.

3. (A)　(B)　(C)
4. (A)　(B)　(C)
5. (A)　(B)　(C)
6. (A)　(B)　(C)

「特殊な文」は固定表現！一度覚えたら楽勝！

Part 3 Short Conversations   DL 138, 139   CD3-23 ~ CD3-27

Listen to a short conversation, and choose the best answer to each question.

7. Where is this conversation taking place?
- (A) In an office
- (B) At a bank
- (C) In a court
- (D) At a seminar

> 会話の「場所」
> →冒頭から推測しよう

8. What is the problem?
- (A) The brochures have not arrived.
- (B) The proposal is turned down.
- (C) The details are not finalized yet.
- (D) The software hasn't updated properly.

> トラブル／問題は、
> 「マイナス」のコメントを聞こう！

9. What does the woman want the man to do?
- (A) Get legal advice
- (B) Expand business with the client
- (C) Announce some news
- (D) Get a document signed

> 女性の「要望」は何？

Part 4 Short Talks   DL 140, 141   CD3-28 ~ CD3-31

Listen to a short talk, and choose the best answer to each question.

10. What is the main topic of the report?
- (A) A fall in the employment rate
- (B) A new park will be opened
- (C) The expansion of a business
- (D) The election of a new official

> 報告の「主題」
> → 冒頭を聞こう！

11. What is Picos?

> 会社の「業種」を推測！

- (A) A car producer
- (B) A housing firm
- (C) An electrical appliance store
- (D) A local supermarket

12. According to the report, what does the State Governor hope will happen?
- (A) More companies will move in.
- (B) A new financial advisor will come.
- (C) The economy will go into recession.
- (D) Construction will take 50 years.

> 名詞キーワードは
> 必ずチェックしよう！

Unit **14** Business   41

Unit 15
Reception Desk

受付でのやりとりは、ビジネスの定番です。何について話しているのかがわかれば簡単。基本表現を押さえるだけで、リスニング力は各段にアップします。

Part 1　Photographs　　DL 142, 143　CD3-32　CD3-33

Look at the picture and choose the statement that best describes what you see.

1. (A) (B) (C) (D)　　　　　　　　　　**2.** (A) (B) (C) (D)

> 2人の「位置」をチェック！

> 「向き合う」は定番表現！

Part 2　Question-Response　　DL 144～147　CD3-34～CD3-37

Choose the best response to each question or statement.

3. (A)　(B)　(C)
4. (A)　(B)　(C)
5. (A)　(B)　(C)
6. (A)　(B)　(C)

> Would you / Could youの「依頼文」は定番！

Part 3 Short Conversations   DL 148, 149   CD3-38 ~ CD3-42

Listen to a short conversation, and choose the best answer to each question.

7. Where does this conversation most likely take place?
   (A) On the telephone
   (B) At a banquet hall
   (C) At a reception counter
   (D) At an insurance agency

   > 会話の「場所」→ シチュエーションを把握しよう！

8. Who most likely is Mr. Hammond?
   (A) The main secretary
   (B) A receptionist
   (C) A city official
   (D) A company head

   > Who設問
   > →「職業」を見抜け！

9. What will the woman do next?
   (A) Telephone her family
   (B) Contact the vice-president
   (C) Speak to a client
   (D) Make a delivery

   > do next →
   > I'll ~のパターンに気付こう！

Part 4 Short Talks   DL 150, 151   CD3-43 ~ CD3-46

Listen to a short talk, and choose the best answer to each question.

10. When will the business open again?
    (A) 7 a.m. the next day
    (B) 8:30 a.m. the next day
    (C) 5 p.m. in the evening
    (D) The day after tomorrow

    > 「日時」や「曜日」は
    > 言い換えに注意！

11. What can visitors to the location enjoy tomorrow?
    (A) A drink at a café
    (B) A drive around the town
    (C) A meal on the course
    (D) A party at a club

    > 「プラス」の内容を
    > キャッチしよう！

12. How can listeners book the services offered?
    (A) By buying lunch from the restaurant
    (B) By turning up early in the morning
    (C) By registering online at any time
    (D) By calling again after 6 p.m.

    > 予約の「方法」は？

Unit 16
Office Work

オフィスでは、様々なトピックに対応しなければなりません。会議、研修、人事、販売戦略、キャンペーンなど、トピックを意識することが大事です。

Part 1　Photographs　　DL 152, 153　CD3-47　CD3-48

Look at the picture and choose the statement that best describes what you see.

1. (A) (B) (C) (D)　　　　　　　　2. (A) (B) (C) (D)

「動作」チェックを忘れずに！

男性の「位置」を確認しよう！

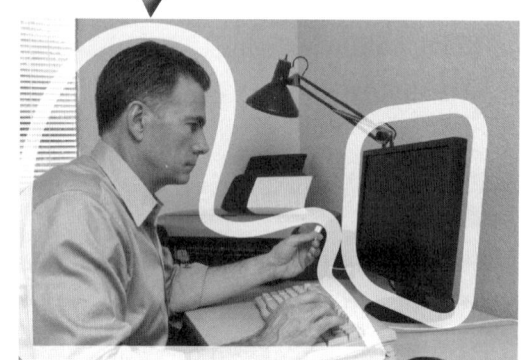

Part 2　Question-Response　　DL 154～157　CD3-49～CD3-52

Choose the best response to each question or statement.

3. (A)　(B)　(C)
4. (A)　(B)　(C)
5. (A)　(B)　(C)
6. (A)　(B)　(C)

「依頼文」への変則的な応答に注意！

Part 3 Short Conversations 🎧 DL 158, 159 ⊙ CD3-53 ~ ⊙ CD3-57

Listen to a short conversation, and choose the best answer to each question.

7. Why will the timecard system change?
   (A) To replace a broken machine
   (B) To improve the current system
   (C) To save more money
   (D) To manage employees better

   > システムを変える「理由」とは？

8. What must be written by hand with the current system?
   (A) Order collections
   (B) Mistakes
   (C) Worker names
   (D) Adjustments

   > 設問のポイントを見抜こう！
   > by handを待ち伏せ！

9. How does the man probably feel about the new system?
   (A) Excited
   (B) Sad
   (C) Nervous
   (D) Uncertain

   > 「感情」問題は、プラス／マイナスで判断！

Part 4 Short Talks 🎧 DL 160, 161 ⊙ CD3-58 ~ ⊙ CD3-61

Listen to a short talk, and choose the best answer to each question.

10. Who most likely is the speaker?
    (A) A product designer
    (B) A company executive
    (C) A radio host
    (D) An advertising agent

    > 「話し手」は誰？
    > 意外な人物であることも！

11. What happened on March 23?
    (A) A store was established.
    (B) A product was bought out.
    (C) An item went on sale.
    (D) A newspaper was published.

    > 「日付」「数字」は、耳印にしよう！

12. What are the sales results?
    (A) Less profit than expected
    (B) Much higher than anticipated
    (C) It's a big announcement
    (D) The same as last year

    > セールの「結果」は？
    > アナウンスの後半から推測！

Unit 16 Office Work   45

Unit 17
Employment & Personnel

人事はビジネスパーソンの一大事。昇任、転勤(異動)、退職、採用面接、新人研修など、人事トピックは豊富です。就任・退職スピーチも常連ですね。

Part 1　Photographs

DL 162, 163　CD3-62　CD3-63

Look at the picture and choose the statement that best describes what you see.

1. (A) (B) (C) (D)　　　2. (A) (B) (C) (D)

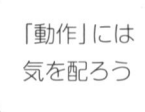

「共通点」は何？

「動作」には気を配ろう

Part 2　Question-Response

DL 164 ~ 167　CD3-64 ~ CD3-67

Choose the best response to each question or statement.

3. (A)　(B)　(C)
4. (A)　(B)　(C)
5. (A)　(B)　(C)
6. (A)　(B)　(C)

「間接疑問文」の「疑問詞」をキャッチ！

Part 3 Short Conversations   DL 168, 169   CD3-68 ~ CD3-72

Listen to a short conversation, and choose the best answer to each question.

7. Why did the man contact the woman?
   (A) To apply to a job position
   (B) To inquire about finances
   (C) To respond to an application
   (D) To return a telephone call

   > Why設問→「理由」をキャッチ！

8. When will the speakers most likely meet?
   (A) Tuesday morning
   (B) Tuesday afternoon
   (C) Wednesday morning
   (D) Wednesday afternoon

   > most likely →「推測」のサイン

9. According to the man, what should the woman bring to the meeting?
   (A) A claim form
   (B) Nothing in particular
   (C) A questionnaire
   (D) Job references

   > ミーティングに持ってくる「モノ」は何？

Part 4 Short Talks   DL 170, 171   CD3-73 ~ CD3-76

Listen to a short talk, and choose the best answer to each question.

10. How many months has Nathan Monday set a sales record?
    (A) Two months
    (B) Four months
    (C) Five months
    (D) Six months

    >「数字」問題はトリッキー！

11. What does the speaker say Nathan Monday has done since he was hired?
    (A) Surpassed monthly sales targets
    (B) Hired employees
    (C) Gave an achievement award
    (D) Represented his department

    > 人名＝名詞キーワード！

12. What will the participants do next?
    (A) Keep up the good work
    (B) Report new sales figures
    (C) Go to the stage
    (D) Listen to a speech

    > 定番の do next！
    > スピーチの最後を聞こう

Unit 17 Employment & Personnel   47

Unit 18
Office Announcement

オフィスアナウンスは、社内連絡のようなものです。社内の工事案内、会議やパーティの案内、旅費規程の改定など、社員へのお知らせと思えば簡単ですね。

Part 1　Photographs　　DL 172, 173　CD3-77　CD3-78

Look at the picture and choose the statement that best describes what you see.

1. (A) (B) (C) (D)　　　　　　　2. (A) (B) (C) (D)

「ガランとした部屋」は何て言う？

2人の「位置」関係をチェック！

Part 2　Question-Response　　DL 174～177　CD3-79 ～ CD3-82

Choose the best response to each question or statement.

3. (A)　(B)　(C)
4. (A)　(B)　(C)
5. (A)　(B)　(C)
6. (A)　(B)　(C)

「平叙文」への様々な応答に対応しよう

Part 3 Short Conversations   DL 178, 179   CD3-83 ~ CD3-87

Listen to a short conversation, and choose the best answer to each question.

7. What will be happening in the office tomorrow?
   (A) The speakers will work overtime.
   (B) Electricians will come in.
   (C) The office will close at 9 p.m.
   (D) The manager will have a meeting.

   明日の「出来事」→
   会話の未来表現にヒント！

8. What is the problem for the two speakers?
   (A) They haven't received the documents.
   (B) They will do some repair work.
   (C) They have to complete the work tonight.
   (D) The computer needs to be fixed.

   トラブル／問題を把握しよう！
   「マイナス」要素をキャッチ！

9. What will the woman most likely do after this?
   (A) Call her spouse   (C) Talk to the repair person
   (B) Send an e-mail   (D) Go straight home

   定番のdo (next)！
   会話の最後にヒント、だね

Part 4 Short Talks   DL 180, 181   CD3-88 ~ CD3-91

Listen to a short talk, and choose the best answer to each question.

10. What does the speaker remind listeners about today?
    (A) A school will be opened.
    (B) Many customers are coming.
    (C) An arts festival will be held.
    (D) The center will close early.

    remind = tellとすれば簡単！
    設問のリーディングは大事！

11. Who is Jackie Dee?
    (A) A famous musician
    (B) A family member
    (C) A regular customer
    (D) A well-known writer

    定番のWho設問！
    →「職業」を聞こう

12. What does the speaker suggest available staff do at 3 p.m.?
    (A) Gather for a meeting
    (B) Sign up for overtime
    (C) Do a stock-take
    (D) Help with crowd control

    どんなstaff？
    availableの解釈を間違えるな！

Unit **18** Office Announcement

Unit 19
Office Talk

オフィストークは、ビジネスからプライベートに至るまで、様々な内容が含まれます。同僚とのおしゃべりをイメージすればわかりやすいでしょう。

Part 1　Photographs　DL 182, 183　CD4-02　CD4-03

Look at the picture and choose the statement that best describes what you see.

1. (A) (B) (C) (D)　　　　2. (A) (B) (C) (D)

3人でも「共通点」をチェック！

「向き合う」は出るぞ！

Part 2　Question-Response　DL 184～187　CD4-04 ～ CD4-07

Choose the best response to each question or statement.

3. (A)　(B)　(C)
4. (A)　(B)　(C)
5. (A)　(B)　(C)
6. (A)　(B)　(C)

平叙文の応答にはくせ者が多い！

Part 3 Short Conversations   DL 188, 189   CD4-08 ~ CD4-12

Listen to a short conversation, and choose the best answer to each question.

7. What problem are the speakers discussing?
   (A) A repairman hasn't come yet.
   (B) There are too many printed materials.
   (C) A photocopier doesn't work well.
   (D) The manager doesn't work on the projects.

   > オフィストラブルは日常茶飯事！

8. What does the man say he should request the manager to do?
   (A) Call a repair person
   (B) Get a new machine
   (C) Take more frequent breaks
   (D) Print out materials

   > 男性の「要望」は？ managerがキーワード！

9. According to the man, how can people work efficiently?
   (A) By being in good health
   (B) By having control over projects
   (C) By using a printer regularly
   (D) By keeping office equipment in good shape

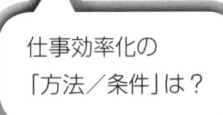

   > 仕事効率化の「方法／条件」は？

Part 4 Short Talks   DL 190, 191   CD4-13 ~ CD4-16

Listen to a short talk, and choose the best answer to each question.

10. What is the main purpose of the announcement?
    (A) To advertise an apartment
    (B) To inform changes in rules
    (C) To redesign the staff room
    (D) To explain new facilities

    > アナウンスの「目的」！冒頭をチェック

11. Why has the new room been offered for the staff?
    (A) To arrange for lunch
    (B) To shorten work hours
    (C) To provide a space for smokers
    (D) To increase work performance

    > 「理由」をしっかりキャッチしよう

12. Who will have to keep the area clean?
    (A) The managers   (C) Every staff member
    (B) A cleaning service   (D) New employees

    > 設問にヒントを探そう！本文解釈のヒントは設問にアリ！

Unit **19** Office Talk

Unit 20
New Products

(新)製品については、店頭ディスプレイや工場写真が定番です。
オフィスでの売上トークや店頭の販売トークに加え、ラジオCMなどでも扱われます。

Part 1　Photographs　　DL 192, 193　CD4-17　CD4-18

Look at the picture and choose the statement that best describes what you see.

1. (A) (B) (C) (D)　　　　2. (A) (B) (C) (D)

ギッシリの棚は定番！

「展示」では arrange や display を待ち伏せよう

Part 2　Question-Response　　DL 194 ~ 197　CD4-19 ~ CD4-22

Choose the best response to each question or statement.

3. (A)　(B)　(C)
4. (A)　(B)　(C)
5. (A)　(B)　(C)
6. (A)　(B)　(C)

応答が「疑問文」のパターンをマスターしよう！

Part 3 Short Conversations DL 198, 199 CD4-23 ~ CD4-27

Listen to a short conversation, and choose the best answer to each question.

7. Who are the two speakers?
   (A) Package designers
   (B) Restaurant workers
   (C) Department colleagues
   (D) Food manufacturers

   > 話し手の「職業」をイメージして！

8. How will the product name be decided?
   (A) By public vote
   (B) Through TV advertising
   (C) By matching it to other product names
   (D) By asking the employees

   > 製品の名前の「決め方」は？今回のHowは難しいぞ！

9. What will the woman most likely do next?
   (A) Enter a competition
   (B) E-mail workers for their ideas
   (C) Make the product package
   (D) Test the taste of the food

   > 定番のdo next！そろそろ完璧かな？

Part 4 Short Talks DL 200, 201 CD4-28 ~ CD4-31

Listen to a short talk, and choose the best answer to each question.

10. Who is this talk mainly aimed at?
    (A) Customers interested in the outdoors
    (B) Engineers at a product show
    (C) Fans of freshly brewed beverages
    (D) Specialty magazine readers

    > トークの「対象」は誰？冒頭から推測しよう！

11. How is the Vega different from other products?
    (A) It uses a certain type of water.
    (B) Drinks are ready in less than a couple of minutes.
    (C) The price has been reduced.
    (D) It has a grinder inside.

    > 商品(Vega)の独自性は何？「違い」を述べた箇所を聞こう

12. How can listeners purchase the Vega?
    (A) By visiting a certain café where it is stocked
    (B) By going to a kitchen appliance store
    (C) By ordering it online
    (D) From a mail order catalog

    > 購入方法を聞こう！

Unit **20** New Products

Unit 21
Sales

TOEICはセールが大好き。いつもセールをしている印象があります。
店頭のセール写真やトーク、販売戦略に関するオフィストークが頻出です。

Part 1   Photographs   DL 202, 203   CD4-32   CD4-33

Look at the picture and choose the statement that best describes what you see.

1. (A) (B) (C) (D)   **2.** (A) (B) (C) (D)

「見る」は lookだけではない

「展示」の頻出表現は？

Part 2   Question-Response   DL 204 ~ 207   CD4-34 ~ CD4-37

Choose the best response to each question or statement.

3. (A) (B) (C)
4. (A) (B) (C)
5. (A) (B) (C)
6. (A) (B) (C)

「提案・勧誘」のレギュラー表現をマスターしよう！

Part 3 Short Conversations DL 208, 209   CD4-38 ~ CD4-42

Listen to a short conversation, and choose the best answer to each question.

7. Where is the conversation probably taking place?
   (A) At a department store
   (B) At a restaurant
   (C) At a post office
   (D) At a newspaper stand

   会話の「場所」は冒頭！

8. What is the problem with the coupon?
   (A) It is out of date.
   (B) Spending needs to be over a certain amount.
   (C) It can only be used at a certain branch.
   (D) A member's card is needed.

   クーポンの「問題」は何？

9. What does the woman suggest the man do?
   (A) Become a member
   (B) Buy the goods today
   (C) Visit another branch
   (D) Subscribe to a paper

   女性の「提案」をキャッチしよう
   会話の最後に注意して！

Part 4 Short Talks DL 210, 211   CD4-43 ~ CD4-46

Listen to a short talk, and choose the best answer to each question.

10. In what type of business is the speaker working?
    (A) A grocery store
    (B) A health-oriented eatery
    (C) A vegetable farming
    (D) A gift center

    どんなビジネス＝「業種」？

11. What is one of the new items being offered?
    (A) A fruit juice   (C) A variety of snack bars
    (B) A hot herbal tea   (D) An iced yogurt

    新商品は何？
    設問をシンプルに
    理解して！

12. How do customers receive a free gift?
    (A) By making a one-time purchase
    (B) By giving a product review
    (C) By using a coupon
    (D) By showing proof of multiple visits

    free giftの受取方法は？
    How設問は必ずゲット！

Unit **21** Sales 55

Unit 22

Seminar & Meeting

会議やセミナーは、ビジネスと相性抜群。会議写真はおなじみですね。ですが、会議室でのビジネストークは多岐に及ぶので注意が必要です。

Part 1　Photographs　DL 212, 213　CD4-47　CD4-48

Look at the picture and choose the statement that best describes what you see.

1. (A) (B) (C) (D)　　　　2. (A) (B) (C) (D)

> 全員の「共通点」を見よう！

> イスの「並び」に注目！

Part 2　Question-Response　DL 214～217　CD4-49～CD4-52

Choose the best response to each question or statement.

3. (A)　(B)　(C)
4. (A)　(B)　(C)
5. (A)　(B)　(C)
6. (A)　(B)　(C)

> 〈否定疑問文 → 難応答〉に対応できる力をつけよう

Part 3 Short Conversations　　DL 218, 219　　CD4-53 ~ CD4-57

Listen to a short conversation, and choose the best answer to each question.

7. What is going to start on Thursdays?
   (A) Trips abroad
   (B) An exchange program
   (C) Language classes
   (D) Art lessons

> 講座／クラスの種類を見抜こう

8. Why is the woman reluctant to attend the course?
   (A) She's never studied French.
   (B) She doesn't want to go on her own.
   (C) She's forgotten what she learned.
   (D) She doesn't have much time.

> 女性が気の進まない理由は何？

9. What does the man suggest the woman do?
   (A) Visit Paris
   (B) Register full-time
   (C) Wait three months
   (D) Attend the class

> 男性の「提案」をキャッチ！

Part 4 Short Talks　　DL 220, 221　　CD4-58 ~ CD4-61

Listen to a short talk, and choose the best answer to each question.

10. Who is the talk addressed to?
   (A) New company employees
   (B) Investors in the organization
   (C) Leaders in the community
   (D) Columbus committee

> トークの「対象」は？設問の意味をとらえて！

11. What will HIO direct their attention to this year?
   (A) Enriching the surrounding community
   (B) Expanding after-school programs
   (C) Growing the company in new markets
   (D) Holding workshops about community service

> HIOは何に注目している？

12. What most likely will happen next?
   (A) The speakers will introduce themselves.
   (B) The attendees will begin to leave.
   (C) A question and answer session will start.
   (D) The workshops will start.

> 「次の展開」は、トークの最後を聞こう！

Unit **22** Seminar & Meeting

Unit 23
Logistics

運輸・流通は、倉庫写真や在庫トークに顕著です。
交通トピックとも関連するので、頻出表現はまとめて覚えておくと便利です。

Part 1　Photographs　　DL 222, 223　CD4-62　CD4-63

Look at the picture and choose the statement that best describes what you see.

1. (A) (B) (C) (D)　　　　　2. (A) (B) (C) (D)

「箱が積まれている」は何て言う？

「埠頭」も出るぞ！

Part 2　Question-Response　　DL 224 ~ 227　CD4-64 ~ CD4-67

Choose the best response to each question or statement.

3. (A)　(B)　(C)
4. (A)　(B)　(C)
5. (A)　(B)　(C)
6. (A)　(B)　(C)

「How」は頻出！
ヴァリエーションをチェック！

Part 3 Short Conversations   DL 228, 229   CD4-68 ~ CD4-72

Listen to a short conversation, and choose the best answer to each question.

7. What is the purpose of the call?
(A) To sell office materials
(B) To store important documents
(C) To inquire about a price quote
(D) To receive company details

電話の「目的」！
→ セオリー通り、冒頭にヒント！

8. What will happen to the filing cabinets?
(A) They will be removed while remodeling.
(B) Someone will keep them in the store.
(C) A repair person will fix them.
(D) They will stay where they are.

名詞キーワードをチェックしよう！

9. What does the man say he will do next?
(A) Revise the prices
(B) Increase the cost
(C) Move cabinets
(D) Find an old estimate

定番の do next！→ 取りこぼし厳禁！

Part 4 Short Talks   DL 230, 231   CD4-73 ~ CD4-76

Listen to a short talk, and choose the best answer to each question.

10. What type of business is the speaker working in?
(A) An insurance agency
(B) An academic institute
(C) A staff training company
(D) A professional moving company

仕事のジャンルは、
選択肢「タテ読み」が効果的

11. What is the reason for the insurance?
(A) To cover the cost of travel
(B) To pay for lost or damaged property
(C) To help with employment costs
(D) To assist with medical expenses

キーワードを耳印に、ヒントを聞こう

12. Who can get discounts?
(A) Workers to be transferred overseas
(B) New graduates
(C) Students entering college
(D) Company employees

割引の「対象者」は誰？

Unit 23 Logistics 59

Unit 24

Construction & Production

TOEICは工事や作業が大好き。工事現場や野外作業の写真に加え、社内工事や公共施設の改修トークなど、ガテン系トピックが頻出です。

Part 1　Photographs　　DL 232, 233　CD4-77　CD4-78

Look at the picture and choose the statement that best describes what you see.

1. (A) (B) (C) (D)　　　　**2.** (A) (B) (C) (D)

「カートを押す」のヴァリエーション！

「重機」は定番表現！

Part 2　Question-Response　　DL 234 ~ 237　CD4-79 ~ CD4-82

Choose the best response to each question or statement.

3. (A)　(B)　(C)
4. (A)　(B)　(C)
5. (A)　(B)　(C)
6. (A)　(B)　(C)

さあ、「疑問詞」の最終チェックをしよう！

Part 3 Short Conversations   DL 238, 239   CD4-83 ~ CD4-87

Listen to a short conversation, and choose the best answer to each question.

7. What will happen on the 19th?
   (A) There will be no gas.
   (B) The street will be blocked.
   (C) The woman won't use her car.
   (D) A neighborhood party will take place.

   「日付」を耳印に、その周辺を聞こう

8. What did the man give the woman?
   (A) A complimentary pass
   (B) A parking fine
   (C) A resident card
   (D) A recommendation letter

   男性が手渡したモノは？

9. What does the man suggest the woman do?
   (A) Arrange for paid parking
   (B) Leave home early
   (C) Move the vehicle a day before
   (D) Take alternative transport

   難設問のsuggest！男性の「提案」を聞こう！

Part 4 Short Talks   DL 240, 241   CD4-88 ~ CD4-91

Listen to a short talk, and choose the best answer to each question.

10. What is the main purpose of the talk?
    (A) To notify that building work will affect business
    (B) To inform of complaints from customers
    (C) To request closure of the building
    (D) To remind staff of a change in the transport system

    トークの「目的」！冒頭以外にヒントがあるケースも！

11. What is the problem with Maypole Street?
    (A) There is no parking available.
    (B) Customers have to use the East gate.
    (C) The door of the entrance can't be opened.
    (D) There will be construction vehicles parked on it.

    キーワードを耳印に、「トラブル／問題」をキャッチ！

12. What does the speaker want employees to do?
    (A) Meet clients at other locations
    (B) Help visitors choose a service
    (C) Tell customers about building access
    (D) Contact the construction company

    wantの設問！話し手の「要望」は何？

Unit 24 Construction & Production   61

本書には CD（別売）があります

STRIKE UP THE TOEIC® TEST LISTENING
解法のコツを学ぶ TOEIC®テストリスニング演習

2015 年 1 月 20 日　初版第 1 刷発行
2022 年 2 月 20 日　初版第 10 刷発行

著　者　　塚　田　幸　光

発行者　　福　岡　正　人
発行所　　株式会社　金　星　堂

（〒101-0051）東京都千代田区神田神保町 3-21
Tel.（03）3263-3828（営業部）
　　（03）3263-3997（編集部）
Fax（03）3263-0716
http://www.kinsei-do.co.jp

編集担当　西田碧　　　　　　　　　　Printed in Japan
印刷所・製本所／三美印刷株式会社

本書の無断複製・複写は著作権法上での例外を除き禁じられています。本書を代行業者等の第三者に依頼してスキャンやデジタル化することは、たとえ個人や家庭内での利用であっても認められておりません。

落丁・乱丁本はお取り替えいたします。

ISBN978-4-7647-4005-1　C1082

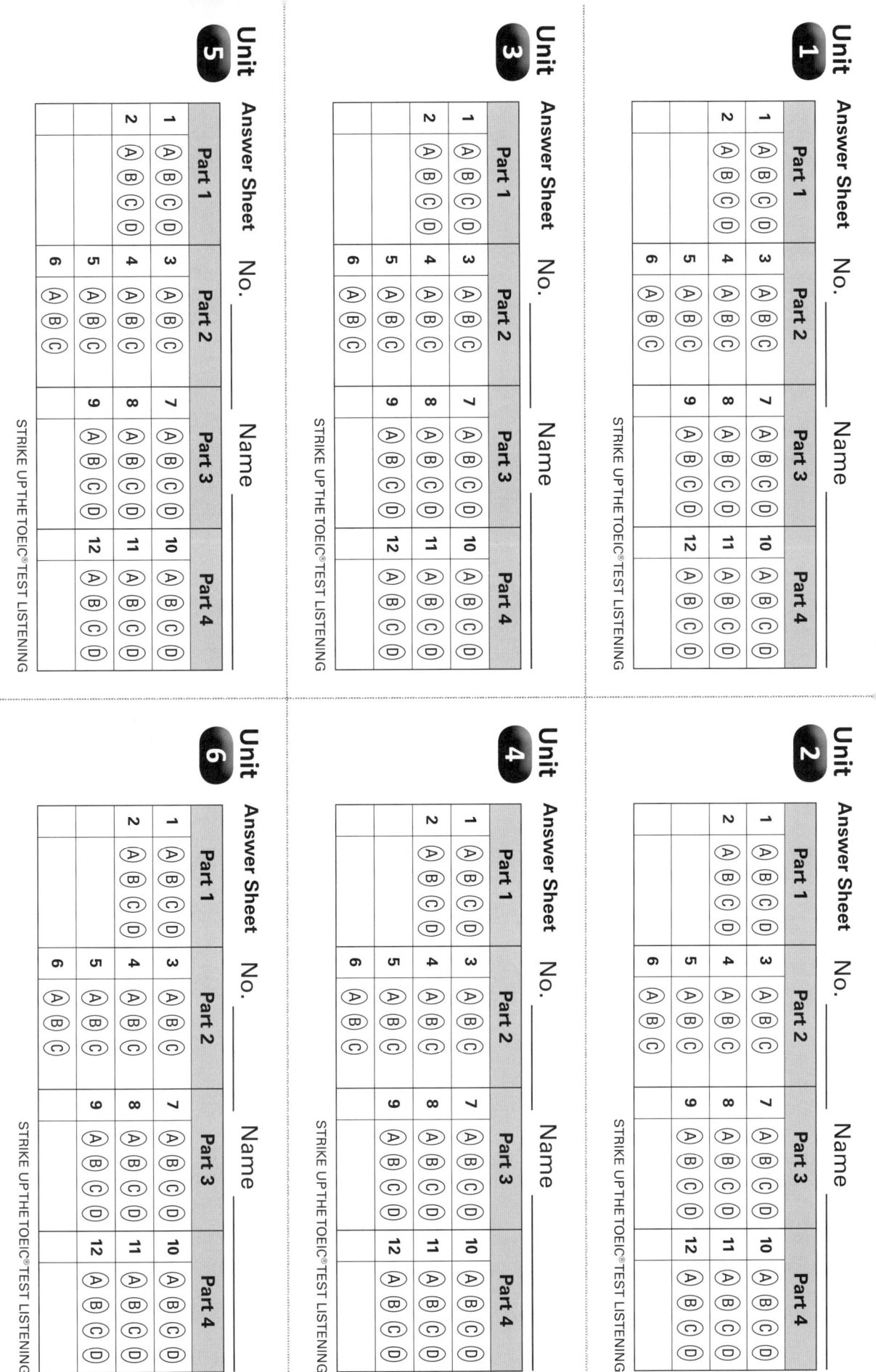

Unit 1 — Answer Sheet   No. _____   Name _____

Part 1		Part 2		Part 3		Part 4	
1	Ⓐ Ⓑ Ⓒ Ⓓ	3	Ⓐ Ⓑ Ⓒ	7	Ⓐ Ⓑ Ⓒ Ⓓ	10	Ⓐ Ⓑ Ⓒ Ⓓ
2	Ⓐ Ⓑ Ⓒ Ⓓ	4	Ⓐ Ⓑ Ⓒ	8	Ⓐ Ⓑ Ⓒ Ⓓ	11	Ⓐ Ⓑ Ⓒ Ⓓ
		5	Ⓐ Ⓑ Ⓒ	9	Ⓐ Ⓑ Ⓒ Ⓓ	12	Ⓐ Ⓑ Ⓒ Ⓓ
		6	Ⓐ Ⓑ Ⓒ				

STRIKE UP THE TOEIC® TEST LISTENING

Unit 2 — Answer Sheet   No. _____   Name _____

Part 1		Part 2		Part 3		Part 4	
1	Ⓐ Ⓑ Ⓒ Ⓓ	3	Ⓐ Ⓑ Ⓒ	7	Ⓐ Ⓑ Ⓒ Ⓓ	10	Ⓐ Ⓑ Ⓒ Ⓓ
2	Ⓐ Ⓑ Ⓒ Ⓓ	4	Ⓐ Ⓑ Ⓒ	8	Ⓐ Ⓑ Ⓒ Ⓓ	11	Ⓐ Ⓑ Ⓒ Ⓓ
		5	Ⓐ Ⓑ Ⓒ	9	Ⓐ Ⓑ Ⓒ Ⓓ	12	Ⓐ Ⓑ Ⓒ Ⓓ
		6	Ⓐ Ⓑ Ⓒ				

STRIKE UP THE TOEIC® TEST LISTENING

Unit 3 — Answer Sheet   No. _____   Name _____

Part 1		Part 2		Part 3		Part 4	
1	Ⓐ Ⓑ Ⓒ Ⓓ	3	Ⓐ Ⓑ Ⓒ	7	Ⓐ Ⓑ Ⓒ Ⓓ	10	Ⓐ Ⓑ Ⓒ Ⓓ
2	Ⓐ Ⓑ Ⓒ Ⓓ	4	Ⓐ Ⓑ Ⓒ	8	Ⓐ Ⓑ Ⓒ Ⓓ	11	Ⓐ Ⓑ Ⓒ Ⓓ
		5	Ⓐ Ⓑ Ⓒ	9	Ⓐ Ⓑ Ⓒ Ⓓ	12	Ⓐ Ⓑ Ⓒ Ⓓ
		6	Ⓐ Ⓑ Ⓒ				

STRIKE UP THE TOEIC® TEST LISTENING

Unit 4 — Answer Sheet   No. _____   Name _____

Part 1		Part 2		Part 3		Part 4	
1	Ⓐ Ⓑ Ⓒ Ⓓ	3	Ⓐ Ⓑ Ⓒ	7	Ⓐ Ⓑ Ⓒ Ⓓ	10	Ⓐ Ⓑ Ⓒ Ⓓ
2	Ⓐ Ⓑ Ⓒ Ⓓ	4	Ⓐ Ⓑ Ⓒ	8	Ⓐ Ⓑ Ⓒ Ⓓ	11	Ⓐ Ⓑ Ⓒ Ⓓ
		5	Ⓐ Ⓑ Ⓒ	9	Ⓐ Ⓑ Ⓒ Ⓓ	12	Ⓐ Ⓑ Ⓒ Ⓓ
		6	Ⓐ Ⓑ Ⓒ				

STRIKE UP THE TOEIC® TEST LISTENING

Unit 5 — Answer Sheet   No. _____   Name _____

Part 1		Part 2		Part 3		Part 4	
1	Ⓐ Ⓑ Ⓒ Ⓓ	3	Ⓐ Ⓑ Ⓒ	7	Ⓐ Ⓑ Ⓒ Ⓓ	10	Ⓐ Ⓑ Ⓒ Ⓓ
2	Ⓐ Ⓑ Ⓒ Ⓓ	4	Ⓐ Ⓑ Ⓒ	8	Ⓐ Ⓑ Ⓒ Ⓓ	11	Ⓐ Ⓑ Ⓒ Ⓓ
		5	Ⓐ Ⓑ Ⓒ	9	Ⓐ Ⓑ Ⓒ Ⓓ	12	Ⓐ Ⓑ Ⓒ Ⓓ
		6	Ⓐ Ⓑ Ⓒ				

STRIKE UP THE TOEIC® TEST LISTENING

Unit 6 — Answer Sheet   No. _____   Name _____

Part 1		Part 2		Part 3		Part 4	
1	Ⓐ Ⓑ Ⓒ Ⓓ	3	Ⓐ Ⓑ Ⓒ	7	Ⓐ Ⓑ Ⓒ Ⓓ	10	Ⓐ Ⓑ Ⓒ Ⓓ
2	Ⓐ Ⓑ Ⓒ Ⓓ	4	Ⓐ Ⓑ Ⓒ	8	Ⓐ Ⓑ Ⓒ Ⓓ	11	Ⓐ Ⓑ Ⓒ Ⓓ
		5	Ⓐ Ⓑ Ⓒ	9	Ⓐ Ⓑ Ⓒ Ⓓ	12	Ⓐ Ⓑ Ⓒ Ⓓ
		6	Ⓐ Ⓑ Ⓒ				

STRIKE UP THE TOEIC® TEST LISTENING

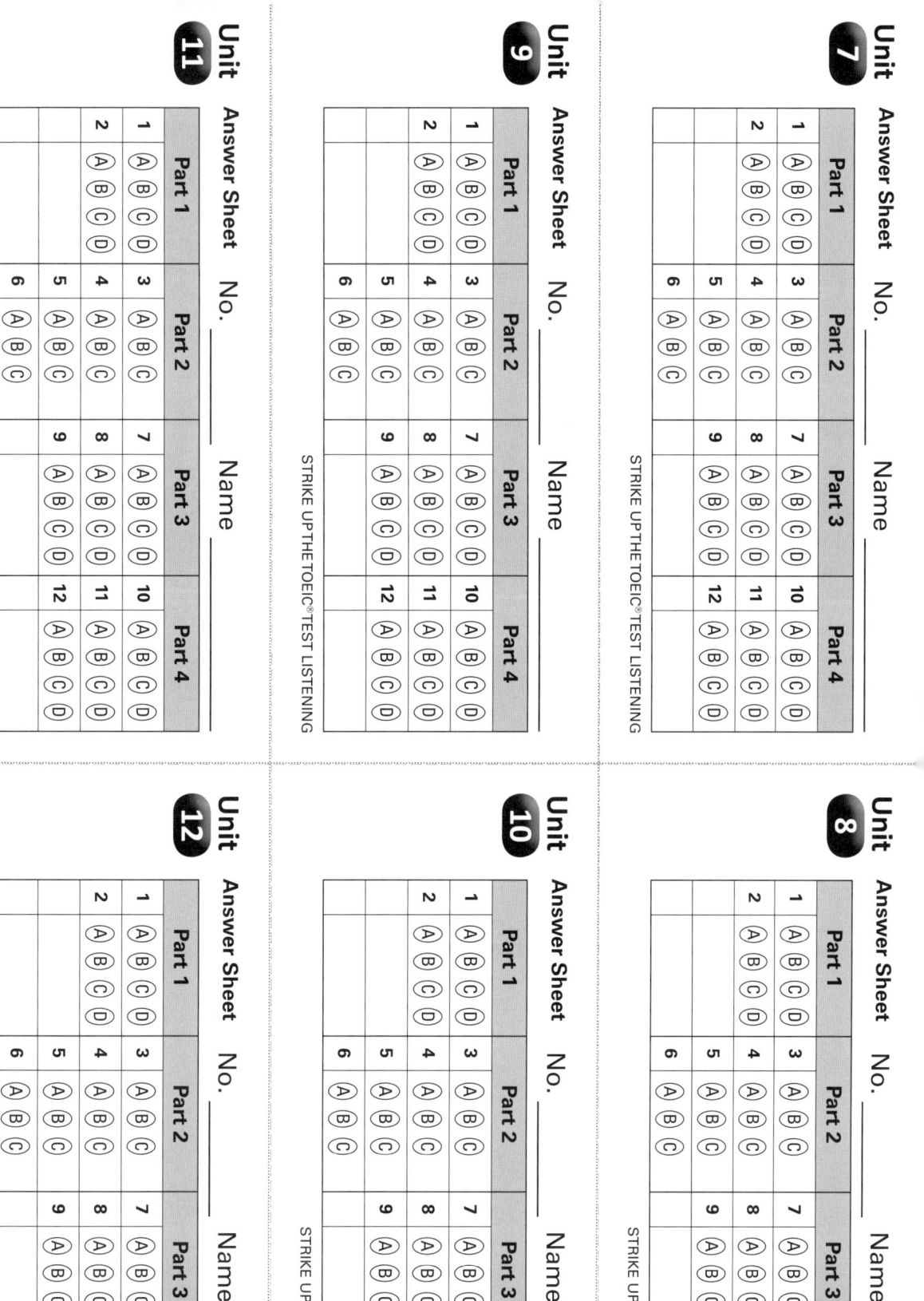

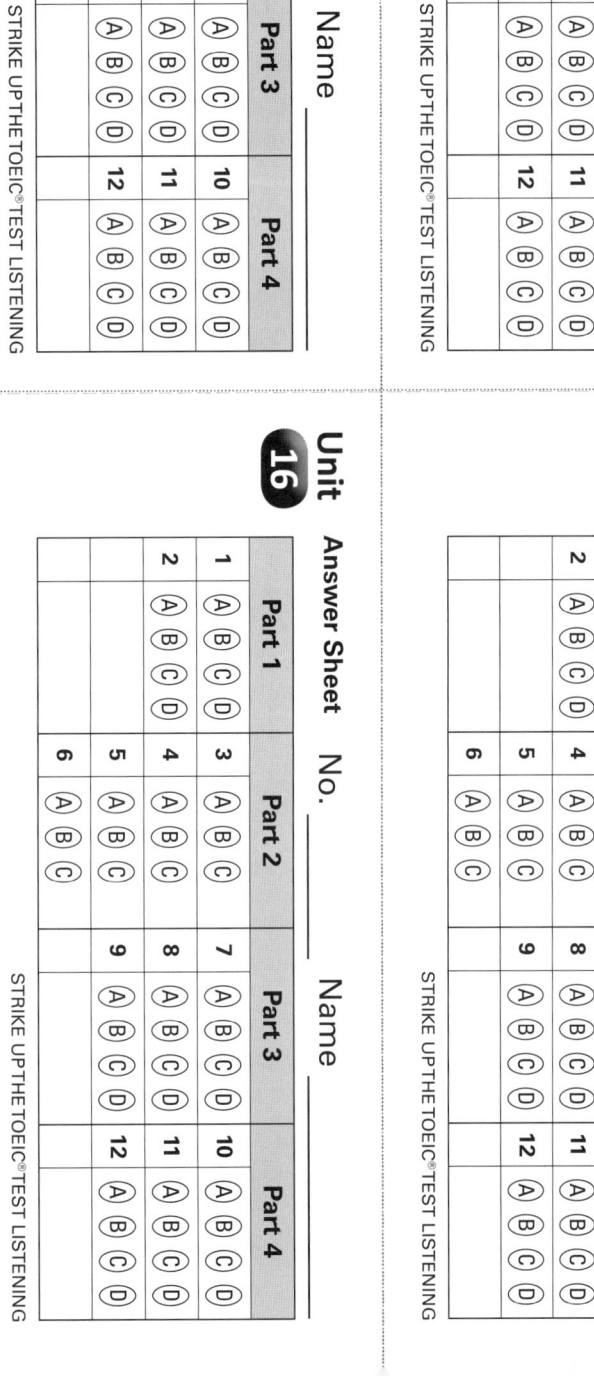

Answer Sheets

Unit 13
No. _____ Name _____

Part 1				Part 2			Part 3				Part 4			
1	Ⓐ Ⓑ Ⓒ Ⓓ	3	Ⓐ Ⓑ Ⓒ	7	Ⓐ Ⓑ Ⓒ Ⓓ	10	Ⓐ Ⓑ Ⓒ Ⓓ
2	Ⓐ Ⓑ Ⓒ Ⓓ	4	Ⓐ Ⓑ Ⓒ	8	Ⓐ Ⓑ Ⓒ Ⓓ	11	Ⓐ Ⓑ Ⓒ Ⓓ
		5	Ⓐ Ⓑ Ⓒ	9	Ⓐ Ⓑ Ⓒ Ⓓ	12	Ⓐ Ⓑ Ⓒ Ⓓ
		6	Ⓐ Ⓑ Ⓒ				

STRIKE UP THE TOEIC® TEST LISTENING

Unit 14
No. _____ Name _____

Part 1	Part 2	Part 3	Part 4
1 Ⓐ Ⓑ Ⓒ Ⓓ	3 Ⓐ Ⓑ Ⓒ	7 Ⓐ Ⓑ Ⓒ Ⓓ	10 Ⓐ Ⓑ Ⓒ Ⓓ
2 Ⓐ Ⓑ Ⓒ Ⓓ	4 Ⓐ Ⓑ Ⓒ	8 Ⓐ Ⓑ Ⓒ Ⓓ	11 Ⓐ Ⓑ Ⓒ Ⓓ
	5 Ⓐ Ⓑ Ⓒ	9 Ⓐ Ⓑ Ⓒ Ⓓ	12 Ⓐ Ⓑ Ⓒ Ⓓ
	6 Ⓐ Ⓑ Ⓒ		

STRIKE UP THE TOEIC® TEST LISTENING

Unit 15
No. _____ Name _____

Part 1	Part 2	Part 3	Part 4
1 Ⓐ Ⓑ Ⓒ Ⓓ	3 Ⓐ Ⓑ Ⓒ	7 Ⓐ Ⓑ Ⓒ Ⓓ	10 Ⓐ Ⓑ Ⓒ Ⓓ
2 Ⓐ Ⓑ Ⓒ Ⓓ	4 Ⓐ Ⓑ Ⓒ	8 Ⓐ Ⓑ Ⓒ Ⓓ	11 Ⓐ Ⓑ Ⓒ Ⓓ
	5 Ⓐ Ⓑ Ⓒ	9 Ⓐ Ⓑ Ⓒ Ⓓ	12 Ⓐ Ⓑ Ⓒ Ⓓ
	6 Ⓐ Ⓑ Ⓒ		

STRIKE UP THE TOEIC® TEST LISTENING

Unit 16
No. _____ Name _____

Part 1	Part 2	Part 3	Part 4
1 Ⓐ Ⓑ Ⓒ Ⓓ	3 Ⓐ Ⓑ Ⓒ	7 Ⓐ Ⓑ Ⓒ Ⓓ	10 Ⓐ Ⓑ Ⓒ Ⓓ
2 Ⓐ Ⓑ Ⓒ Ⓓ	4 Ⓐ Ⓑ Ⓒ	8 Ⓐ Ⓑ Ⓒ Ⓓ	11 Ⓐ Ⓑ Ⓒ Ⓓ
	5 Ⓐ Ⓑ Ⓒ	9 Ⓐ Ⓑ Ⓒ Ⓓ	12 Ⓐ Ⓑ Ⓒ Ⓓ
	6 Ⓐ Ⓑ Ⓒ		

STRIKE UP THE TOEIC® TEST LISTENING

Unit 17
No. _____ Name _____

Part 1	Part 2	Part 3	Part 4
1 Ⓐ Ⓑ Ⓒ Ⓓ	3 Ⓐ Ⓑ Ⓒ	7 Ⓐ Ⓑ Ⓒ Ⓓ	10 Ⓐ Ⓑ Ⓒ Ⓓ
2 Ⓐ Ⓑ Ⓒ Ⓓ	4 Ⓐ Ⓑ Ⓒ	8 Ⓐ Ⓑ Ⓒ Ⓓ	11 Ⓐ Ⓑ Ⓒ Ⓓ
	5 Ⓐ Ⓑ Ⓒ	9 Ⓐ Ⓑ Ⓒ Ⓓ	12 Ⓐ Ⓑ Ⓒ Ⓓ
	6 Ⓐ Ⓑ Ⓒ		

STRIKE UP THE TOEIC® TEST LISTENING

Unit 18
No. _____ Name _____

Part 1	Part 2	Part 3	Part 4
1 Ⓐ Ⓑ Ⓒ Ⓓ	3 Ⓐ Ⓑ Ⓒ	7 Ⓐ Ⓑ Ⓒ Ⓓ	10 Ⓐ Ⓑ Ⓒ Ⓓ
2 Ⓐ Ⓑ Ⓒ Ⓓ	4 Ⓐ Ⓑ Ⓒ	8 Ⓐ Ⓑ Ⓒ Ⓓ	11 Ⓐ Ⓑ Ⓒ Ⓓ
	5 Ⓐ Ⓑ Ⓒ	9 Ⓐ Ⓑ Ⓒ Ⓓ	12 Ⓐ Ⓑ Ⓒ Ⓓ
	6 Ⓐ Ⓑ Ⓒ		

STRIKE UP THE TOEIC® TEST LISTENING

Unit 19 Answer Sheet   No. _____   Name _____

Part 1		Part 2		Part 3		Part 4	
1	A B C D	3	A B C	7	A B C D	10	A B C D
2	A B C D	4	A B C	8	A B C D	11	A B C D
		5	A B C	9	A B C D	12	A B C D
		6	A B C				

STRIKE UP THE TOEIC® TEST LISTENING

Unit 20 Answer Sheet   No. _____   Name _____

Part 1		Part 2		Part 3		Part 4	
1	A B C D	3	A B C	7	A B C D	10	A B C D
2	A B C D	4	A B C	8	A B C D	11	A B C D
		5	A B C	9	A B C D	12	A B C D
		6	A B C				

STRIKE UP THE TOEIC® TEST LISTENING

Unit 21 Answer Sheet   No. _____   Name _____

Part 1		Part 2		Part 3		Part 4	
1	A B C D	3	A B C	7	A B C D	10	A B C D
2	A B C D	4	A B C	8	A B C D	11	A B C D
		5	A B C	9	A B C D	12	A B C D
		6	A B C				

STRIKE UP THE TOEIC® TEST LISTENING

Unit 22 Answer Sheet   No. _____   Name _____

Part 1		Part 2		Part 3		Part 4	
1	A B C D	3	A B C	7	A B C D	10	A B C D
2	A B C D	4	A B C	8	A B C D	11	A B C D
		5	A B C	9	A B C D	12	A B C D
		6	A B C				

STRIKE UP THE TOEIC® TEST LISTENING

Unit 23 Answer Sheet   No. _____   Name _____

Part 1		Part 2		Part 3		Part 4	
1	A B C D	3	A B C	7	A B C D	10	A B C D
2	A B C D	4	A B C	8	A B C D	11	A B C D
		5	A B C	9	A B C D	12	A B C D
		6	A B C				

STRIKE UP THE TOEIC® TEST LISTENING

Unit 24 Answer Sheet   No. _____   Name _____

Part 1		Part 2		Part 3		Part 4	
1	A B C D	3	A B C	7	A B C D	10	A B C D
2	A B C D	4	A B C	8	A B C D	11	A B C D
		5	A B C	9	A B C D	12	A B C D
		6	A B C				

STRIKE UP THE TOEIC® TEST LISTENING